UNEARTHED

UNEARTHED

The Source Behind Elite Performance

Ed Tseng
Best-Selling Author • TEDx Speaker • Pro of the Year

Invisible **Edge Publishing**

Copyright © 2026 Edward Tseng

All rights reserved.

No part of this book may be reproduced, stored in a retrieval system, or transmitted in any form or by any means—electronic, mechanical, photocopying, recording, or otherwise—without prior written permission from the publisher, except for brief quotations used in reviews.

Published by Invisible Edge Publishing, Lawrenceville, NJ

ISBN: 979-8-218-92698-4 (Paperback)

Printed in the United States of America

Disclaimer:

This book is for informational and educational purposes only. It is not medical advice and is not intended to diagnose, treat, cure, or prevent any condition. Always seek advice from a qualified professional regarding any medical or psychological concerns. The author and publisher assume no responsibility for errors, omissions, or outcomes related to the use of this material.

DEDICATION

To Ava and Max, my greatest teachers...
for reminding me what matters most,
and for showing me—again and again—
that happiness is not something we chase.

It's something already inside us.
Always.

ACKNOWLEDGEMENTS

No book is ever written alone.

Even when it looks like one person typing late at night, the truth is—there are many voices behind every page. People who shaped the author, challenged the author, loved the author, and reminded the author who he really is.

First, thank you to my children, **Ava and Max**.

You are my greatest joy, my greatest motivation, and I savor every moment I spend with you both. You've shown me what presence looks like. You've shown me what real connection looks like. And you've taught me, in the simplest ways, what I spent years trying to learn as an adult.

Ava—thank you for your strength, your fire, your heart, and your wisdom beyond your years. The words you once said to me—**"You're happy NOW, daddy."**—are not just a parenting moment I'll never forget. They are the heartbeat of this entire book. You reminded me of something I already knew… but had temporarily forgotten.

Maxwell—thank you for your warmth, your gentleness, your humor, and your big heart. You remind me every day that the best parts of life aren't earned through pressure—they appear through love.

You've taught me what resilience looks like.
And you are living proof that we are **born mentally tough**—before the world ever teaches us to doubt ourselves.

To my older sisters, **Grace and Lucy**, for your unending support... and for all the childhood memories (except the ones involving dressing me up as a doll). Just kidding — I love you both.

To my mother, **Mary**, in heaven — you taught me how to love unconditionally, how anyone can be tough as nails, and how to plan for the future but live completely in the now.

To my father, **Vincent**, in heaven — thank you for always pushing me with, "Edward, you need to work hard!" when I failed out of college twice... and later, after I was named Pro of the Year, saying, "Ed... don't work so hard!!!" A beautiful full-circle moment.

Mom and Dad — I will always continue to try to make you proud.

Thank you to the athletes, performers, and clients who trusted me with your stories. Your courage is what shaped these chapters. Every time you opened up about pressure, fear, doubt, and big moments... you helped me see the invisible mechanics of the mind more clearly. This book exists because you were willing to look inward.

Thank you to the coaches, parents, and leaders who care enough to keep learning. You are the quiet heroes of elite performance. You don't just develop skills—you develop people.

I also want to express deep gratitude to **Special Olympics** and everyone involved in the Special Olympics community. Being part of this mission has been one of the great honors of my life. The athletes, coaches, family members and volunteers I've met through Special Olympics are living proof of what this book teaches: that courage is not the absence of pressure, and resilience is not something we earn —

it's something we're born with. Thank you for reminding me what pure joy, presence, and fearless effort really look like.

To **Dr. Rob Gilbert**, who helped me kick off this incredible mindset journey: Your dedication and heart to help others is more impactful than you will ever know.

I also want to acknowledge the mentors and teachers who helped deepen my understanding of how the human experience works from the inside-out. You didn't simply teach me information. You helped me see.

And now I am seeing with a fresh set of eyes—and am forever grateful for that. And finally, thank you to every reader who picked up this book.

If something in these pages resonated with you, it's because you already knew it on some level. My hope is that this book simply helped you remember—and that it opened a door.

Even if just a crack.

TABLE OF CONTENTS

Chapter 1 — The Moment That Exposes Everything

Chapter 2 — Why Mental Strategies Don't Stick

Chapter 3 — Inside-Out: The Single Most Important Truth

Chapter 4 — Clarity Isn't Earned—It Appears

Chapter 5 — Confidence Is Not a Feeling (And That's Good News)

Chapter 6 — Pressure Is Created... Not Caused

Chapter 7 — The Two Voices (Mind vs Personal Thought)

Chapter 8 — The Opponent You Never Trained For—Meet the Characters in Your Head

Chapter 9 — Trusting Training: Letting Skill Execute

Chapter 10 — How to Perform Better Without Trying to Perform Better

Chapter 11 — Coaching & Leading From the Inside-Out

Chapter 12 — The Game Within the Game (Ripple Effect)

Chapter 13 — The Invisible Edge: A New Identity

AUTHOR'S NOTE

This book was written for anyone who has ever felt their performance shrink under pressure.

For anyone who has ever overthought a moment that mattered.

For anyone who has ever believed they needed to "fix themselves" to become consistent.

I wrote this because I've watched performers suffer unnecessarily — not from lack of skill... but from misunderstanding of how the mind works.

My hope is that what you'll find here is not another strategy.

But a deeper understanding.

One that brings you back to clarity.

Back to freedom.

Back to yourself.
Yours from the source —

INTRO — **The Invisible Edge**

There's a moment that every high performer knows.

It's the moment when time slows down — not in the magical way you see in highlight reels, but in the heavy way that feels like your body is moving through water. Your heart is pounding. Your mind is racing. And suddenly you're thinking about everything... except what you've trained your whole life to do.

You step to the line.
You stand over the putt.
You deliver the pitch.
You walk into the meeting.
You sit down for the exam.
You hit "send" on the message that might change everything.

And in that moment, the pressure feels real.

Not theoretical. Not motivational-poster "embrace it" real.

I mean real like you can taste it.

Your stomach tightens.
Your hands feel different.
Your timing is off.
You start trying to be confident.

And then — almost without warning — you begin performing like you've never trained.

Some people call it choking.

But that word never felt fair to me.

Because it assumes you're weak.

It assumes you didn't want it badly enough.

It assumes you weren't mentally tough.

In reality, the people who struggle most under pressure are often the ones who care the most.

They're the most prepared.
They're the most committed.
They're the most driven.

And when the moment arrives… their talent doesn't vanish.

Their talent gets covered.

Covered by thought.
Covered by tension.
Covered by the invisible noise of the mind.

That's what this book is about.

Because after years of working with athletes, leaders, and students — people who are objectively talented and deeply motivated — I've seen a pattern that's as surprising as it is liberating:

The moments that feel like they "break" us aren't actually caused by the moment.

They're created from the inside-out.

And here's the twist:

Pressure isn't the problem. It's the signal.

The Turning Point

For a long time, I did what most of us do.

I tried to solve pressure with strategies:

-Try to think positive

-Visualize success

-Use mantras

-Take deep breaths

-"Get confident"

-"Grind"

-"Control your emotions"

-"Be mentally tough"

And sometimes those things helped... or so I thought.

But what always frustrated me was this:

If strategies were the answer, why did the pressure keep coming back?

Why did confidence feel like it could disappear overnight?

Why did clarity come and go?

Why did some days feel like you were "in the zone," while other days felt like you were battling your own mind?

Then I encountered an understanding that completely changed my work — and my life.

Not a technique.

Not a mental trick.

Not another strategy.

A **truth**.

A truth that high performers brush up against forever... but rarely learn how to explain:

**Your experience is not created from the outside-in.
It's created from the inside-out.**

Pressure Isn't Coming From Your Life

We're taught — explicitly or implicitly — that life creates our experience.

Big game = pressure
Important meeting = stress
Final exam = anxiety
Deadline = more stress

It sounds logical.

It feels true.

And yet... it doesn't hold up under honest observation.

Because if the outside world were creating your experience, then:

-everyone would feel the same pressure in the same moments

-confident people would always feel confident

-nervous people would always feel nervous

-stressful situations would automatically create stress

But that's not what happens.

Some people feel alive in big moments.

Some people feel crushed.

Some feel calm.

Some feel shaky.

The same moment... different experiences.

So what's really going on?

Here's the simplest answer I can give you:

The moment isn't creating the pressure.

Your thinking is.

Not as a choice. Not as your fault. Not because you're doing something wrong.

Just because that's how the human mind works.

Thought creates experience.

And once you truly understand that, something incredible happens:

You stop trying to manage pressure...

...and you start seeing through it.

The Invisible Edge

It's not hype.

It's not aggression.

It's not forcing confidence.

It's understanding where confidence comes from.

It's recognizing thoughts for what they are — momentary mental events... not commands, not prophecies, not truth.

And when a performer sees this...

they stop living at the mercy of their inner weather.

They begin to trust what they've trained to do.

They return to instinct.

They execute with more freedom.

They perform with more joy.

Not because life got easier...

but because they found the *source*.

That's the Invisible Edge — and this book is about unearthing it.

Who This Book Is For

This book is for you if you've ever said:

>-"I'm great in practice but not in games."

>-"I know what to do — I just can't do it when it matters."

>-"My confidence disappears."

>-"I overthink everything."

>-"I feel like I'm fighting myself."

>-"I just want to be free out there."

Athletes. Business leaders. Students. Performers.

Anyone who wants to perform with more freedom — and live with more peace.

What Will Change For You

This book won't give you 26 mental tricks.

It'll give you something better:

A deeper understanding of what's creating your experience.

When you understand the inside-out nature of experience

    -your mind settles more quickly

    -you stop taking thoughts so seriously

    -confidence becomes more consistent

    -pressure becomes lighter

    -and your best execution shows up more often aka the zone

You won't feel fearless.

You'll feel free.

And that's the *real* edge.

CHAPTER 1 — The Moment That Exposes Everything

There's a strange moment that happens right before pressure takes over.

It's not loud.
It's not dramatic.
Most people won't even notice it happening.

But if you've ever struggled in big moments, you know exactly what I mean.

You're standing there... and everything is normal.

And then—suddenly—it's not.

Your mind shifts.

It starts doing what minds do.

It begins scanning the future like a security guard:

What if I mess this up?
What if everyone sees?
What if this changes things?
What if I don't live up to what they expect?
What if I'm not as good as they think?
What if I let them down?
What if I let myself down?

And before you've even made a move, the moment feels heavier.

Not because the moment actually changed…

…but because your **thinking** did.

The Myth of "Choking"

We call it choking.

That word carries judgment. It implies weakness.

But what if choking isn't a character flaw?

What if it's simply what happens when a human mind misunderstands what's happening inside itself?

Because the performers who struggle most in big moments are rarely lazy.

Usually… they're the ones who care the most.

They're invested.

And caring does something interesting to the mind:

It turns "this matters" into "this is dangerous."

Pressure Has a Pattern

Whether it's sports, business, or school, the internal experience is often identical.

At first, you're fine.

Then the mind tries to protect you.

Don't screw up.

That thought carries a message:

This moment threatens your identity.

And once identity is involved, everything becomes personal.

The Most Important Question

When pressure shows up, most people ask:

"How do I get rid of this feeling?"

But there's a more powerful question:

"Where does pressure come from?"

Because once you understand pressure… it starts losing its grip.

Pressure isn't the opponent.
Pressure isn't the stakes.
Pressure isn't the audience.

Pressure is what happens when thinking becomes more believable.

The mind creates meaning.

Meaning creates experience.

The Trap: Trying to Fix Yourself

When pressure hits, performers often believe the feeling means something is wrong.

So they try to fix it.

Force calm.
Force confidence.
Force focus.

And that effort creates more thinking → more pressure → more tightness.

Here's the truth:

You're not broken.

You're human.

The Slump That Changed Everything

A baseball player once told me about a slump that nearly broke him.

He was 0-for-20.

Zero hits in twenty at-bats.

To say he was struggling would be an understatement.

And like most high-level athletes, he didn't respond by relaxing.

He responded by trying to fix himself.

He changed his stance.
His grip.
His stride.
His timing.
His approach.

He tried everything.

His coaches tried.
His teammates tried.
Everybody had a suggestion.

But nothing changed—because the problem was never mechanical.

It was *mental*.

Identity had gotten involved.

And then one day, after weeks of effort, he hit a breaking point.

He told himself:

"I give up. I'm going to stop trying."

Not because he quit...

...but because he finally stopped fighting his own mind.

That night, he got three hits.

Just like that, the slump ended.

Not because he found some new secret...

...but because the noise cleared, and what was always there showed up again.

Not long after, he got called up to the major leagues.

And this is the part most people miss:

He didn't "get his confidence back."

He stopped trying to manufacture it.

The Insight

Big moments don't break you.

They reveal what you believe about your inner world.

If you believe the moment creates your feelings... you'll live at the mercy of the moment.

But if you understand the inside-out truth, pressure becomes a signal:

"My mind is creating more meaning right now. And that is completely normal."

And once you see that...

...you stop fighting it.

Your Invisible Edge

Pressure doesn't come from the moment.

Pressure is created by the mind's interpretation of the moment.

The stakes don't cause pressure.

Thought does.

And if thought creates pressure...

...it can't be as powerful as it looks.

Your best isn't missing.

It's closer than you think.

源

Next: CHAPTER 2 — Why Mental Strategies Don't Stick

Most performers don't struggle because they lack discipline.
They struggle because they're trying to use strategies to control something that's already coming from within.
In the next chapter, we'll explore why mental strategies don't stick— and what does.

CHAPTER 2 — Why Mental Strategies Don't Stick

If you've ever struggled under pressure, chances are you've tried to fix it.

You've tried to fix yourself.

Not because you're weak.
Not because you're broken.

Because you're human.
And because you care.

So you do what high performers always do: you search for a solution.

You learn techniques.

You collect mental strategies like tools in a toolbox:

Positive self-talk. Visualization. Breathing. Mantras. Routines, "confidence hacks."
Focus cues. Mindset training. Gratitude lists. Mental toughness drills.

And sometimes… they help. Or at least it seems that way.

And that's what makes this so confusing.

Because on Monday, you do the routine—and you feel great.

You feel focused. Calm. Confident.

Then on Friday, with the same routine, in the same body...

...it's gone.

Pressure returns.
Doubt returns.
Tightness creeps in.

And you find yourself thinking:

"Why isn't this working anymore?"

Or worse:

"What's wrong with me?"

The Hidden Trap

Most mental strategies are built on one assumption:

Your feelings are the problem.

They assume pressure is something that shouldn't be there.
They assume doubt is dangerous.
They assume nerves mean you're not ready.

So the whole system becomes:

If I feel something I don't like... I must control it.

And once you start trying to control your internal world…

…you create a second performance.

One external.
One internal.

And that internal scoreboard is exhausting.

A tennis player once called me, frustrated.

"This mental stuff isn't working!"

"What mental stuff?" I asked.

"The stuff you teach me. I know thinking gets in my way. I know I'm at my best when I have clarity. But today I was on court… thinking about whether my thinking was good or not."

Silence.

Then laughter.

She said, "Of course I wasn't playing well—because thinking about your thinking is *still* thinking."

"And any thinking outside the moment is the opposite of clarity… and the zone."

Why Strategies Work... Then Stop Working

To be fair, strategies can work—but only when they come from your own insight, not someone else's ideas or strategy.

Breathing can interrupt thinking.
A routine can create familiarity.
A cue can settle the body.

But the mistake is believing the strategy created your confidence.

It didn't.

It simply created a moment of quiet—where confidence and clarity could show up again.

So now you need it.

And once you need it...

...you're not free.

Then when the strategy fails, you panic.

But here's the truth:

Confidence is not created by a technique.

Confidence is created by understanding—understanding how the mind works.

The Insight

You don't need better thoughts.

You need a better understanding of thought. A better understanding of what is creating your experience.

Because when you understand thought...

you stop taking it personally.
you stop treating it like truth.
you stop wrestling with it.
you stop fearing feelings.

You become freer.

Your Invisible Edge

Most mental strategies don't stick because they solve the wrong problem.

They try to control experience.

But experience doesn't need control.

It needs understanding.

You don't need to defeat pressure.

You need to see where it's coming from.

Not from the moment.

From *thought* in the moment.

源

Next: CHAPTER 3 — Inside-Out: The Single Most Important Truth

Every performer wants the same thing: to feel free in the moment and to play to their potential.
But freedom doesn't come from controlling the mind.
It comes from understanding where experience is actually coming from—the inside-out.

CHAPTER 3 — Inside-Out: The Single Most Important Truth

If you only read one chapter of this book, it should probably be this one.

Because it contains the understanding that changes *everything*:

All experience is created from the inside-out.

That sentence may sound simple.

But once you truly see what it means, pressure stops being mysterious... and performance stops feeling fragile.

Because the truth is:

Pressure isn't caused by the moment.
It's created by thinking that feels true.
The moment is neutral.
Meaning makes it heavy.
And meaning comes from thought.

Why This Matters More Than Anything Else

Most performers spend their whole lives trying to fix the outside.

The opponent.
The environment.
The stakes.

The crowd.
The conditions.

And when they can't control those things...

They turn inward.

They try to control their mind.
They try to control their feelings.
They try to manage confidence like it's something they can manufacture on command.

But that entire approach is built on a misunderstanding:

That life happens outside-in.
That the moment creates your experience.
That pressure is "out there."
That confidence is something you either have... or lose.

And if you don't have it, you have to fight your way back.

But that's not how the mind works.

The Hidden Trap

If you believe the moment creates your feelings...

You will always be at the mercy of the moment.

Because in big moments, the mind will always create more meaning.

It can't help it.

A championship point.
A big meeting.
A tryout.
A test.
An interview.

The mind sees importance and instantly turns it into danger.

Not because the moment is dangerous…

…but because the mind begins predicting and protecting.

So pressure shows up.

Not as a choice.

As a human experience.

And the more you misunderstand it, the more personal it becomes.

You start believing the feeling means something is wrong.

You start believing your thoughts.

You start believing you're losing something.

And that is when performance tightens.

Inside-Out: The Single Most Important Truth

All experience is created from the inside-out.

That means the moment isn't creating your pressure.

Thought is creating your experience of the moment.

It doesn't mean the outside world isn't real.

It means the feeling you live in always comes from one place:

Your thinking in the moment.

When thought is calm, the moment feels calm.
When thought speeds up, the moment feels heavier.
When thought feels threatening, the moment feels dangerous.

Same moment.
Different experience.

Why?

Because the mind is the projector.

And the world is the screen.

The Story That Made This Real

A hockey player I met after a lecture once confided in me that he had been in a deep depression for six years.

Therapy wasn't helping.
Medication wasn't helping.

So right there—in the restaurant—we talked.

Nothing dramatic.

Just a human conversation.

A week later I received a voicemail.

"Ed, ever since we met... for the first time in six years, I've gone to bed smiling... and I've woken up smiling."

Then he said:

"In the past, I thought if I went on vacation, I would snap out of it. I went to an island... and my depression followed me there."

"Then I moved to a warm climate, thinking paradise would fix it. It followed me there too."

"And now I realize something."

"Our experience of life is like the Bob Marley lyric: You're running and running and running away... but you can't run away from yourself."

"I still feel depressed sometimes. We all do. But now I know it's just coming from depressed thinking... or a depressed memory."

"And it comes and goes... instead of being in my face for six years."

Over time, this young man continued to improve.

Eventually, with his doctor, he came off medication.

He no longer felt the need for therapy.

Today, he's one of the most optimistic people I've ever met.

I've seen this same truth show up far beyond one conversation... and far beyond one sport.

Rick Down—former hitting coach for the New York Yankees—reached out to me years ago because he was curious about the way I approached the mental game.

I did have a book at the time.
I was known to a degree.

But Rick wasn't looking for hype.

He was past his prime in professional baseball, yet his passion to help the next generation had never faded.

We talked often about performance, pressure, and thinking.

One theme kept coming up.

Even world champions get caught up in their thinking.

Just like everyone else.

Not because they're broken.
Not because they're flawed.

But because they're human.

And when you understand how the mind actually works...

You stop trying to fix people.

You start pointing them back to themselves.

Confidence Doesn't Vanish

This is one of the most freeing things you'll ever realize:

Confidence doesn't vanish.

It doesn't get destroyed by pressure.
It doesn't disappear forever.
It doesn't get "lost."

It gets covered.

Covered by noisy thinking.
Covered by meaning.
Covered by identity.
Covered by fear.

That's why a performer can look unstoppable in warmups…

…and feel completely different once the "real moment" begins.

Not because their talent left.

Because the mind got louder.

And when the mind gets louder, access gets covered.

Pressure Revisited

Pressure is real as an experience.

You feel it in your chest.
In your breathing.
In your timing.

In your body.

But pressure is not real as a cause.

It isn't proof that the moment is dangerous.

It's proof the mind is creating meaning.

Meaning creates experience.

That's why pressure can show up during practice.

That's why the same athlete can feel free one day... and tight the next.

Same environment.
Different meaning.
Different thinking.
Different experience.

If you put 100 people in front of a large crowd, would all 100 feel pressure?

No.

Some would be excited.
Some would barely care.
Some would feel alive.

If the situation caused feelings, everyone would feel the same.

They don't.

So something else must be creating experience.

Nightmares and "Daymares"

In dreams, your heart races.

Your body reacts.

It feels real.

Then you wake up.

Nothing happened.

It was thinking.

We understand nightmares.

But we don't realize we do the same thing during the day.

We have daymares.

The mind imagines a future.

Replays a memory.

Creates a scenario.

And the body reacts as if it's happening now.

Once you see this...

You stop treating thinking like a threat.

You stop treating feelings like emergencies.

You stop fighting your inner world.

And suffering decreases.

Not because pain disappears.

But because you stop adding resistance.

The Insight

Pressure doesn't mean you're weak.
Pressure doesn't mean you're not ready.
Pressure doesn't mean something is wrong.

It means your mind is creating more meaning right now.

And when you see that...

Pressure starts losing its grip.

Not because you fought it.

But because you stopped believing the illusion that the moment is doing this to you.

Your Invisible Edge

You don't need to change the moment.

You need to understand what's creating your experience of the moment.

Pressure isn't caused by the moment.

It's created by the voice about the moment.

And when thought settles...

Your natural confidence resurfaces.
Your timing returns.
Your skill comes back.
Your best performance shows up again.

Without force.

Because your best isn't something you create.

It's something you return to.

This is the game within the game.

The invisible shift beneath performance.

Elite performance may be what brought you here.

But what stays...

Is something even bigger—**A better life.**

源

Next: CHAPTER 4 — Clarity Isn't Earned—It Appears

Most performers believe clarity is something you have to *work your way into*.

But clarity isn't earned through effort.

It appears when thinking settles—and you stop fighting your own mind.

CHAPTER 4 — Clarity Isn't Earned—It Appears

Most people think clarity is something you earn.

Something you work hard enough for.
Something you "lock in."
Something you deserve after enough preparation or experience.

And when clarity disappears, we assume we did something wrong.

So we push harder.

We tighten.

We try to force the mind into the "right state."

But clarity isn't something you create.

Clarity is what's left when the noise settles.

The Hidden Trap

The problem isn't that performers don't want clarity.

It's that they believe clarity is a goal to chase.

They treat clarity like a destination:

"If I do enough mental training, I'll finally feel clear."

"If I repeat the right affirmations, I'll feel confident."

"If I stay positive, I'll stay in the zone."

But chasing clarity is the fastest way to lose it.

Because the very act of *trying to force the mind* creates more thinking and clutter.

More effort.
More thinking.
More monitoring.
More evaluating.

And soon you're not just playing the game…

You're **watching** yourself play the game.

The Snow Globe

Think of a shaken snow globe.

That's what the mind can look like under pressure.

Thoughts flying.
Meaning swirling.
Emotion rising.

And when that happens, most performers respond by shaking it more.

They do more.

Think more.

Try more.

They search for the perfect cue… the perfect mantra… the perfect thought…

as if the right thought will restore clarity.

But you can't force clarity by shaking it more.

Clarity returns when the mind settles.

Why Clarity Shows Up When You Stop Trying

Have you ever noticed when your best ideas show up?

Not when you're grinding.

Not when you're forcing.

But when you're *not trying*.

That's why answers arrive:

in the shower,
on a walk,
after sleep,

driving in silence,
doing something ordinary.

Clarity doesn't respond to effort.

Clarity responds to quiet.

Not quiet on the outside...

quiet on the *inside*.

Clarity Isn't Calm

Here's another misunderstanding that traps high performers:

They confuse clarity with calm.

They think:

"If I'm nervous, I can't be clear."

"If I'm excited, I'll be out of control."

"If I feel intensity, I must be losing it."

But clarity isn't calm.

You can be nervous and clear.

You can be fired up and clear.

You can feel your heart pounding and still see everything perfectly.

Clarity is not the absence of sensation.

Clarity is the absence of confusion.

That distinction matters.

Because the moment you stop treating sensation as a problem...

you stop fighting yourself.

And fighting yourself is what creates confusion.

The Performer's Real Job

So what is the performer's job in big moments?

It's not forcing the right mental state.

It's recognizing noise... and not feeding it.

That's it.

Noise might sound like:

What if I miss?
What if I fail?
What if they judge me?
What if I'm not who they think I am?

Noise might show up as:

tightness in the body,
a racing heart,

a spike of fear,
a heavy feeling.

And this is where most people misunderstand what's happening.

They assume the noise is a warning.

So they respond like it's an emergency.

They start arguing with it.

Fixing it.

Resisting it.

Trying to replace it.

And unintentionally...

they keep it alive.

Watch the Best Performers Closely

Next time you see a great performance by an athlete, make it a point to watch the post-game interview.

Most certainly, the interviewer will ask:

"How did you play so well?"

And the athlete will almost always look puzzled and reply with something like:

"Uh... I don't know. I was just looking for a good pitch to hit."

The key word is just.

It just happened.

It just flowed.

Notice what they *don't* say.

They don't say:

"Oh, I took a deep breath, said an affirmation, and then forced myself to get in the zone."

Elite performance rarely sounds like a plan.

It sounds like presence.

The athlete simply lets thoughts come and go...

...and returns to the task at hand.

That's the zone.

And here's what most people misunderstand:

The zone is not the absence of thought.

It's the absence of *attachment* to thought.

Thoughts can still appear—just like clouds in the sky.

But clouds don't mean the sun is gone.

The sun is always behind the clouds.

And your confidence is always behind cloudy thinking in the moment.

The Insight

When you stop chasing clarity... clarity appears.

Not because you forced it.

Because you finally stopped blocking it.

The mind settles the way water settles.

Naturally.

On its own.

When it's not being stirred.

And once you see this, you stop asking:

"How do I get to clarity?"

And instead you begin asking:

"Why do I continue to stir the water if it's not helping me?"

That question alone changes everything.

Your Invisible Edge

Clarity isn't earned.

It appears.

Clarity isn't created.

It's what's left when the noise settles.

You can't force clarity by thinking harder.

You can't force the zone by chasing the zone.

The performer's job isn't to manufacture the perfect mental state.

It's to recognize noise…

...and stop feeding it.

When you stop chasing clarity...

clarity appears.

源

Next: CHAPTER 5 — Confidence Is Not a Feeling (And That's Good News)

Most performers believe confidence is something you're supposed to *feel*.

But confidence isn't a feeling you chase—it's a state you return to.

In the next chapter, we'll explore why confidence can be present even when nerves are loud.

CHAPTER 5 — Confidence Is Not a Feeling (And That's Good News)

Confidence is one of the most misunderstood words in performance.

People talk about confidence like it's gasoline—like if you have enough of it, you'll perform well.

And if you don't... good luck.

That's a dangerous belief.

Because the moment confidence becomes a requirement...

performance becomes fragile.

If confidence is required, then you can only perform when you feel a certain way.

And you won't always feel that way.

You're human.

The Hidden Trap

Most performers have been conditioned to believe:

Confidence leads to performance.

So they wait for confidence to show up before they fully commit.

They don't say it out loud, but the mind whispers:

When I feel confident... then I'll go all out.
When I feel ready... then I'll trust my training.
When I feel fearless... then I'll swing freely.

But confidence is not a green light.

Confidence is weather.

It comes.
It goes.
It changes.

And your *ability and effort* does not need to depend on the weather.

Confidence Isn't Required

Here's a simple question:

Have you ever felt nervous... but executed anyway?
Doubted yourself... but still delivered?
Been terrified... but still showed up?

Of course you have.

Which proves something important:

Confidence is not required.

Your performance doesn't depend on feelings.

It depends on something deeper:

Trust.
Freedom.
Clarity.
Understanding.

That's why some of the greatest performances in history weren't performed by someone who felt "confident."

They were performed by someone who stayed present...

even while the mind was loud.

The Elite Lose Confidence Too

I've been fortunate enough to spend time with world champions, gold medalists, business leaders, and even supermodels.

One of the first things I ask them is simple:

"Do you ever lose confidence?"

Every single one of them says yes.

All the time.

Which means something important:

If the elite lose confidence... so will you and so will I.

The difference isn't that they never doubt.

The difference is they don't make it a problem.

They know it's normal.

And they still take action anyway.

Even "Positive Thinking" Can Hurt Performance

The truth is, even "positive thinking" can hurt performance.

Have you ever seen an athlete playing out of their mind?

Everything is flowing. They can't miss. The game looks effortless.

And then they get overly confident.

They start thinking about how well they're playing.

They take their foot off the gas.

They get casual. They get sloppy. They stop doing what was working.

And suddenly the opponent starts coming back... and steals the match.

It happens all the time in sports.

And it happens all the time in life.

Because the problem isn't "negative thinking" or "positive thinking."

The problem is getting pulled into *thinking*—any thinking—outside the moment.

The mind can distract you with fear...

...and the mind can distract you with pride.

Same mechanism. Different costume.

Confidence Is What You Return To

This is the part almost nobody sees:

Confidence is not something you create.

It's something you return to.

Clarity, resilience, confidence, motivation, love—and so many of the "positive feelings" we chase—are closer than we think.

They're not something we have to create.

They are our default.

Think of it like holding a basketball under water.

If you want the ball to float, what do you need to do?

Use affirmations?
A special technique?
A strategy?

Of course not.

You just let go.

Our minds work the same way.

When we're caught in "bad" thinking, the solution isn't to fight it.

It's to see it for what it is:

Just the mind doing what it does—think.

And when you let it be, without wrestling with it...

on its own, it rises back up.

Back to clarity.

Back to flow.

Back to "the zone."

Back to the feeling you were chasing in the first place.

The Insight

So confidence isn't the goal.

It's not the requirement.

And it's not the thing you need to go get before you can perform.

Confidence is simply what tends to be present...

when your mind isn't fighting itself.

That's why trying to "get confident" often backfires.

It quietly reinforces the belief:

Something is missing.

But nothing is missing.

Your ability isn't missing.

Your training isn't missing.

Your best self isn't missing.

It's still there.

It's just covered—like the sun behind clouds.

You Don't Need the Feeling to Take the Action

You don't have to *feel* confident to still take the right action.

Most people don't feel like working out.
Or eating healthy.
Or doing the dishes.

Or making the hard call.
Or having the uncomfortable conversation.

And yet world-class performers do those things anyway.

Not because they have different feelings.

But because they don't make feelings the boss.

Motivation works the same way.

A mentor of mine once told me:

"Motivation is not a feeling. Motivation is an action."

Then he added:

"Winners do what losers don't *feel* like doing."

That's mental toughness.

Not forcing yourself into a feeling…

but refusing to let feelings dictate your behavior.

Your feelings are allowed to come along for the ride.

Your Invisible Edge

Confidence is not a requirement.

Understanding is.

And when you understand where experience comes from...

confidence becomes less important,
doubt becomes less scary,
pressure becomes less powerful,
and performance becomes more natural.

You stop trying to feel ready.

And you start trusting what you've already built.

源

Next: CHAPTER 6 — Pressure Is Created... Not Caused

Most performers believe pressure comes from the situation: the stakes, the opponent, the audience.
But pressure isn't caused by the moment—it's created by our thinking about the moment.
In the next chapter, we'll unpack exactly how that works... and why it sets you free.

CHAPTER 6 — Pressure Is Created... Not Caused

Pressure is real.
But it isn't caused by the moment.
Pressure is created within the moment.

The illusion is this:

"This moment is doing this to me."

But the same moment feels different on different days.
Same stakes.
Different experience.

Which means pressure has a different *source*.

The Hidden Trap

Most performers believe pressure lives in the situation.

The stakes.
The audience.
The opponent.
The consequences.

So when pressure hits, they assume something outside of them must be causing it.

And that assumption makes pressure feel permanent... and personal.

Because if the moment is causing the feeling...

Then the only way out is to change the moment.

But that's virtually impossible.

And that's why pressure feels so suffocating.

Not because it's unstoppable...

...but because it's misunderstood.

The Pressure Recipe

Here's what pressure actually looks like from the inside-out:

A neutral moment appears.
The mind attaches meaning.
Thought speeds up.
Feeling intensifies.

And here's the key:

Believing the thought makes the thought seem truer.

So the mind doubles down.

It starts scanning the future.
It starts protecting your identity.
It starts whispering things like:

Don't mess this up.
This matters.
This changes everything.
What will they think?

But pressure is not about stakes.

Pressure is about meaning.

Meaning makes a moment heavy.

And meaning comes from thought.

Why Pressure Feels So Real

Pressure is real as an experience.

You can feel it in your chest.
In your breathing.
In your timing.
In your body.

But pressure is not real as a cause.

It isn't proof that the moment is dangerous.

It's proof that the mind is creating meaning.

And meaning creates experience.

This is why pressure can show up during practice…

...even when nothing is on the line.

And it's why the same athlete can feel free one day...

...and tight the next.

Same environment.
Different meaning.
Different thinking.
Different experience.

If you took 100 people and asked them to perform in front of a large crowd, would all 100 feel pressure?

Absolutely not.

Of course some would.

But isn't it also true that some would be excited?

Isn't it true that some would barely care at all?

That alone reveals something important:

If an external situation could directly cause how we feel, it would affect everyone the same way. All the time.

But it doesn't.

So something else must be at play here.

I once saw this truth embodied in someone I'll never forget.

Bob Ryland—the first Black professional tennis player and a hero to Arthur Ashe—lived through the segregation we read about in history books.

Not the summarized version.
Not the sanitized version.

The real one.

He went through things no human being should have to experience.

And yet...

Bob was one of the happiest people I've ever known.

Not performatively happy.
Not motivationally happy.

Calm.
Grounded.
Peaceful.

Bob didn't let the outside world determine the quality of his inner world.

He didn't operate from bitterness.
He didn't operate from resentment.

He most certainly could have. I actually gave him my blessing to do so if he wanted to.

But he didn't...

He operated from the inside-out.

Bob went on to coach the Williams sisters and countless other world-class athletes and celebrities.

To me, his greatest achievement wasn't who he coached.

It was who he was.

Bob showed me that circumstances don't create our state of mind.

They reveal *where we're looking from*.

And when you see that clearly...

Pressure stops looking like a monster in the environment.

It starts looking like a misunderstanding in perception.

Most people assume that when pressure shows up, something dangerous is happening.

But what's really happening is much simpler.

The mind is creating a story about a potential future.

And the body is reacting to that story.

Not to reality.
Not to the moment itself.
To thinking.

Once you see this, you stop treating pressure like an enemy.

You start recognizing it as a signal:

"My mind is creating more meaning right now."

And when you recognize that…

Pressure begins to settle on its own.

The Insight

Pressure doesn't mean you're not ready.
Pressure doesn't mean you're weak.
Pressure doesn't mean something is wrong with you.

It means something much simpler:

Your mind is creating more meaning right now.

And once you understand that…

Pressure starts losing its grip.

Not because you fought it…

…but because you stopped believing the illusion that the moment is doing this to you.

Your Invisible Edge

Pressure is real as an experience.

But it is not real as a cause.

Pressure is created by meaning—by thinking—by identity feeling at stake.

And when you understand that...

Pressure loses its grip.

And clarity returns.

Pressure isn't caused by the moment.

It's created by the voice about the moment.

That voice can turn a routine point into a crisis...
a single mistake into a collapse...
and a perfectly neutral situation into a full-blown emergency.

But before we meet the voices...

We need to understand where they come from.

Next: CHAPTER 7 — The Two Voices (Mind vs Personal Thought)

Most people think the voice in their head is their mind.

It isn't.

In the next chapter, you'll explore the difference between the intelligence behind life... and the personal thought that creates mental noise — and why seeing this distinction changes everything.

CHAPTER 7 — The Two Voices (Mind vs Personal Thought)

Most people think the voice in their head is their mind.

It isn't.

One of the most important distinctions you can ever see is this:

There is a difference between the intelligence that gives rise to life...
and the personal thought that creates mental noise.

When those two get lumped together, everything feels complicated.

When they begin to separate, life gets simpler.

Not because you gained control.
Not because you learned a technique.

But because you're no longer mistaking noise for signal.

Beneath personal thought...

There is something quieter.

More stable.

More intelligent.

That deeper level is what we'll call Mind.

Not your brain.
Not your intellect.
Not your memory bank.

Mind is the intelligent life force behind everything that's alive.

It's what grows trees.
It's what heals cuts.
It's what coordinates breathing, digestion, and heartbeat without your involvement.

It's what produces insight.
It's what fuels creativity.
It's what generates intuition.
It's what allows learning to happen.

You don't make any of that occur.

It happens.

Effortlessly.
Automatically.

Because intelligence is built into life.

Including you.

Most people never question where their wisdom comes from.

They just notice that sometimes clarity appears.

An answer pops into mind.
A solution suddenly feels obvious.
A fresh perspective shows up.

They didn't construct it.
They didn't logically assemble it.
They didn't force it.

It arrived.

That arrival point is Mind.

Mind is the *source*.

Personal thought is the content that moves through it.

Personal thought is the voice.

The commentary.
The inner narration.
The opinions.
The judgments.
The stories.
The mental replay.
The mental projection.

It's the part of experience that says:

"What if…"
"I should have…"
"I can't believe…"

"I hope..."
"I'm terrible at this..."
"This always happens..."

That stream is personal thought.

It isn't evil.
It isn't broken.
It isn't your enemy.

It's simply a function.

Just like vision creates images...

Thought creates experience.

The misunderstanding happens when we mistake the noise of personal thought for the intelligence of Mind.

When that happens, we start trying to think our way into wisdom.

We try to analyze our way into peace.

We try to force clarity.

We try to mentally wrestle ourselves into better states.

It rarely works for long.

Because personal thought was never designed to be the source of wisdom.

It was designed to express.

Not lead.

Here's a simple way to feel this distinction.

Think about your best performances.

Not when you were overanalyzing.
Not when you were "in your head."

But when things felt simple.

When actions flowed.
When timing felt natural.
When decisions happened without debate.

In those moments, was your mind noisy?

Usually not.

Personal thought was quieter.

But intelligence was not reduced.

In fact, intelligence was higher.

That's the giveaway.

Clarity does not come from more thinking.

Clarity comes from less interference.

When personal thought settles, Mind becomes more apparent.

Not because it arrived.

But because it was no longer being covered.

It's similar to the sun and clouds.

The sun doesn't turn on when clouds move.

It was already there.

The clouds simply obscured it.

Personal thought is the cloud layer.

Mind is the sun.

You don't need to create the sun.
You don't need to improve the sun.
You don't need to learn how to generate the sun.

You simply need to understand that clouds move.

On their own.

This changes the entire game.

Because you stop trying to "fix" your mind.

You stop treating yourself like a machine that needs constant recalibration.

You stop assuming something is wrong when thinking gets noisy.

You recognize:

"Oh. Thought is active right now."

That's it.

No emergency.
No diagnosis.
No meaning.

And as soon as you stop treating noise as a problem…

It begins to quiet naturally.

Not because you forced it.

But because you removed resistance.

Mind does not get damaged by bad thoughts.

Mind does not disappear under pressure.

Mind does not abandon you after mistakes.

Mind is constant.

Personal thought is variable.

That distinction alone can feel relieving.

It means your access to wisdom, creativity, and clarity is never actually broken.

It only appears blocked when personal thought is loud.

Which is temporary.

Always.

This is why trying to silence our thoughts backfires.

You can't bully clouds into moving.

You don't negotiate with the weather.

You don't argue with the sky.

You allow movement.

The same is true internally.

When you stop fighting personal thought…

It settles faster.

When it settles…

Mind becomes easier to notice.

Not as a booming voice.
Not as a dramatic revelation.

But as a quiet knowing.

A sense of okay-ness.
A subtle clarity.
A feeling of "I've got this."

Athletes often describe this as:

"The game slowed down."
"I just saw it."
"It felt easy."

That isn't personal thought performing miracles.

That's Mind expressing through a quieter system.

Understanding this removes a huge amount of pressure.

Because you realize:

You don't need to manufacture wisdom.
You don't need to construct confidence.
You don't need to build clarity.
You don't need to earn access to your best.

You already have access.

You were born with it.

Your job is not to create intelligence.

Your job is simply not to interfere with it.

Which, paradoxically, takes no effort.

Only understanding.

Once you see the difference between Mind and personal thought…

You stop identifying with every sentence in your head.

You stop assuming every mental comment is meaningful.

You stop obeying every internal suggestion.

Not through discipline.
Not through control.

But through recognition.

You begin to relate to thought the same way you relate to background noise.

Sometimes it's loud.
Sometimes it's quiet.

Either way…

Life continues.

And you continue to function.

From this place…

Performance becomes simpler.
Decision-making becomes simpler.
Mistakes become simpler.

Emotions become simpler.
Life becomes simpler.

Not because you became simplistic.

But because *you're no longer confusing noise with signal.*

Personal thought is noise.

Mind is signal.

And the signal has been broadcasting your entire life.

This chapter isn't here to give you something new.

It's here to point to something familiar.

Something you've already felt.

Those moments of deep clarity.
Those flashes of insight.
Those times when you "just knew."

That wasn't luck.

That wasn't random.

That was Mind.

And it's still there.

Right now—Exactly as it has always been.

源

Next: CHAPTER 8 — The Opponent You Never Trained For

Now that you see the difference between Mind and personal thought...

Let's meet the characters...

CHAPTER 8 — The Opponent You Never Trained For

Meet the Characters in Your Head (and why they're not who you think)

Athletes train for everything.

You train for speed, strength, skill, strategy. You train for weather, bad calls, hostile crowds, momentum shifts... and that one parent in the stands who's yelling like they're on payroll.

You train for opponents.

You even train for pressure moments.

But there's one opponent almost nobody trains for.

Not because it isn't real...

...but because it's invisible.

It can't be scouted. It can't be stretched. You can't outwork it. It travels with you.

And it shows up loudest... when you care the most.

Your biggest opponent is:

The voice in your head.

And here's the twist:

It's not one voice.

It's a cast.

A rotating crew. A full team. A traveling circus.

And when they show up, they don't whisper politely.

They grab the mic.

Meet the Cast

The Evaluator

This character is the MVP.

The Evaluator is the coach you never hired... who somehow got lifetime access to your brain.

One rep and he's like:

"Not good enough."

You could hit a shot that should be on ESPN... and The Evaluator would still find something:

"Nice... but your timing was a little—"

COME ON....

It's exhausting.

The Evaluator doesn't want truth.

He wants commentary.

And the more seriously you take him… the heavier you play.

The Mind Reader

This character is undefeated.

The Mind Reader knows exactly what everyone is thinking…

without evidence.
without data.
without even looking at them.

"Coach thinks I'm soft."
"My teammate is mad at me."
"They're all judging me."

And it's wild because he speaks with so much confidence you forget he's completely making it up.

And here's where you REALLY see it:

Have you ever sent a text… and then read the response and reacted like you're trying to solve a murder mystery?

Seriously…

You text something totally normal.

They text back:

"K."

And suddenly your mind goes:

"OH MY GOD... they're mad."
"What did I do?"
"They never want to talk to me again."
"Should I move?"

And notice...

the moment is neutral.
the text is neutral.

But The Mind Reader turns it into a full-blown Netflix thriller.

The Fortune Teller

The Fortune Teller doesn't predict greatness.

He predicts disaster.

"You're going to miss."
"You're going to choke."
"This isn't going well."

He never says:

"You're about to have the best performance of your life."

No.

He only narrates doom.

And the more you believe him… the more your body tightens… the more you start helping his prediction come true.

The Historian

The Historian keeps receipts.

He shows up mid-game like:

"Remember last time? Let's relive it."

This character replays your worst moments in 4K… at the exact moment you need freedom.

The Historian tries to convince you that the past still exists.

Spoiler: it doesn't.

But it can feel real enough to hijack the present.

The Control Freak

The Control Freak is addicted to certainty.

"I need to feel confident first."
"I need to know it'll work."
"I need to guarantee the outcome."

But sports—life—performance... involve something terrifying:

uncertainty.

The Control Freak wants guarantees.

The game wants courage.

The Spotlight Operator

This character thinks you're on national television.

"Everyone saw that."
"Don't embarrass yourself."

You're at Tuesday practice... and he's acting like you're in the Super Bowl.

The Perfectionist

Perfectionism sounds like excellence…

but it's actually pressure wearing a tuxedo.

"Perfect."
"No mistakes."
"Clean."

But the moment perfection becomes the standard, freedom (and winning) becomes nearly impossible.

The Comparer

This character turns sports into a ranking system.

"He's better."
"She's more natural."
"You're behind."

The Comparer doesn't just compare skills…

he compares worth.

And that's when performance becomes heavy.

The Tragedian

This one deserves its own spotlight.

The Tragedian turns a 2 out of 10 problem...

...into a 12 out of 10 emergency.

He can take a tiny moment... a missed shot, a bad pitch, one awkward rep...

...and turn it into the end of civilization.

And here's what makes The Tragedian so convincing:

The Tragedian weighs zero pounds...

...yet it somehow has the strength of an Olympian...

and the drama of a telenovela.

And it's lifting heavy... while crying.

And suddenly your mind isn't just reacting...

it's performing.

The Big Reveal

Now let's zoom out.

None of these characters are enemies.

They're not real opponents.

They're not your identity.

They are simply:

temporary thought... that seems to be the truth.

The Evaluator isn't truth.
The Mind Reader isn't psychic.
The Fortune Teller isn't a prophet.
The Tragedian isn't accurate.

They're just... characters.

And the most important thing to understand is this:

You don't have to fight them.
You don't have to fix them.
You don't have to "reset."

Because the characters are not the source of performance.

They're not even heavy.

They weigh nothing—They're just loud.

Mic Drop

So the next time you hear one of these characters...

You don't need to panic.

You don't need to argue.

You don't need to negotiate.

You can just smile.

Because now you know what it is.

It's not you.
It's not truth.
It's just a character.

And the best part?

You're not the character.

You're the one *noticing* the character.

And the moment you remember that...

the opponent you never trained for...

loses its power.

Because it was never real.

源

Next: CHAPTER 9 — Trusting Training: Letting Skill Execute

When pressure rises, most performers try to "think" their way back into control.
But performance doesn't improve through more thinking—it improves when training takes over.
In the next chapter, we'll explore how elite performance happens when you stop forcing... and start trusting.

CHAPTER 9 — Trusting Training: Letting Skill Execute

You can spend years building skill…

…and then, in the biggest moment…

you try to do the skill manually.

That's the trap.

Trying creates interference.

And interference blocks execution.

Because execution isn't a thinking skill.

It's a trained skill.

The Hidden Trap

When pressure hits, performers instinctively do what seems logical:

They try harder.
They focus more.
They force more.
They "lock in."

But most of that effort doesn't improve execution.

It interrupts it.

Because training is stored... not remembered.

You don't execute elite performance by thinking your way through it.

You execute elite performance when you allow what you've trained to run.

So the real question becomes:

Can I let what I've trained do the job?

The Story: When Freedom Turns Into Protection

Many years ago, I was working with a young tennis player who had been training hard several days a week.

One day, he decided he wanted to try competing in tournaments.

And in his mind, he had nothing to lose.

So he played loose.

He had fun.

He went after shots.

He trusted what he'd been practicing.

And not only did he have a blast...

he quickly earned a state ranking.

But something changed inside him.

He went from:

"This is fun. What do I have to lose?"

to:

"Oh boy... now I have a ranking. I need to protect it."

Now it mattered.

Now it was personal.

And once his identity got involved, he started thinking more instead of just playing.

He started tightening.

He started managing.

And as quickly as he rose up...

he fell out of the rankings.

Eventually, he reached out to me again.

And that's when he discovered something freeing:

The pressure he felt wasn't coming from his ranking.

It wasn't coming from the matches.

The only thing that changed...

was his thinking.

The Zone Isn't Mysterious

The zone isn't magic.

It's not something you force.

It's not something you "get."

It's simply what performance looks like...

when you stop interfering.

Thinking quiets.

Body takes over.

Training executes.

That's why the best performances often feel strangely simple. Almost like an out of body experience.

Not flashy.

Not complicated—Just clear.

The Insight

Here's the truth:

Tightness isn't proof of anything.

It's not proof you're not ready.

It's not proof you're weak.

It's simply your thoughts getting louder…

…and the body feeling it.

And here's the good news:

You don't have to fight your thoughts to execute.

When you understand where pressure comes from—

when you see thought as just thought—

something settles naturally.

You stop feeding the noise.

As the noise settles…

your attention returns to what's real:

The next rep.
The next pitch.
The next point.

And in that simplicity...

training takes over again.

This is how elite execution works.

Your Invisible Edge

Effort builds skill.

Trust releases skill.

That's elite performance.

源

Next: CHAPTER 10 — How to Perform Better Without Trying to Perform Better

Most people believe improvement comes from effort and control. But in performance, trying harder often creates the very interference you're trying to escape.
In the next chapter, we'll explore the paradox: you play your best when you stop trying to *make* it happen.

CHAPTER 10 — How to Perform Better Without Trying to Perform Better

Most successful high performers eventually learn a counterintuitive truth:

They perform better by trying less.

Not caring less.

Not preparing less.

But forcing less.

That may sound irresponsible at first.

It may even sound lazy.

But it isn't.

It's wisdom.

Because in performance, effort and control are not the same thing.

Effort is how skill is built.

Control is what shows up when fear enters the picture.

The Hidden Trap

When the moment gets big, the mind often gets loud.

And when the mind gets loud, the performer starts trying to manage the experience.

They try to guarantee the outcome.

They try to control their confidence.

They try to control their focus.

They try to control their emotions.

They try to control their swing, their mechanics, their timing.

They become cautious.

They become careful.

They start playing to not lose.

And here's what most people don't realize:

Trying is fear in disguise.

Trying is what happens when the performer believes:

"I need to make sure this goes well."

But the attempt to guarantee the outcome…

is the very thing that pulls you out of the moment.

Why Control Collapses Performance

Control narrows attention.

Control tightens the body.

Control turns performance into monitoring.

Monitoring turns performance into micromanagement.

And micromanagement pulls awareness into the head.

That's why athletes tighten up when they "want it too bad."

That's why presenters sound unnatural when they try to be perfect.

That's why someone can be brilliant in practice…

…and then feel robotic under pressure.

Not because their ability disappeared.

But because fear invited control.

And control displaced presence.

Outcome Attachment

At the psychological level, most interference comes from one place:

Attachment to outcome.

Winning.

Rankings.

Stats.

Approval.

Reputation.

Identity.

When outcome becomes personal…

performance becomes heavy.

Because now every moment is now carrying extra meaning.

"This says something about me."

"This proves something about me."

"This protects something about me."

That weight doesn't make people sharper.

It makes them careful—And careful is rarely free.

What You Can't Control

You cannot fully control winning and losing.

There are too many variables:

Opponents.
Conditions.
Momentum.
Bad calls.
Good bounces.
Luck.

Trying to control the uncontrollable creates tension.

Letting go of control doesn't mean giving up.

It means returning to what's actually in your hands.

Preparation.
Intent.
Competing fully.

That's commitment.

Not control.

The Paradox

Here's the paradox:

The more you try to perform better...

the worse you tend to perform.

Not because effort is bad.

But because trying is psychological control.

And control creates interference.

Effort builds skill.

Control blocks access to skill.

It's like being a race car...

with the emergency brake engaged.

Nothing is wrong with the engine.

You're just creating drag.

Your Invisible Edge

If you want to perform better...

stop trying to perform better.

Not by suppressing effort.

Not by pretending you don't care.

But by recognizing when fear has taken the wheel.

And gently letting go.

Because your best performance isn't a product of control.

It's a product of presence.

It's a product of freedom.

There's an old saying in Chinese philosophy:

Do nothing and get everything.

Not literally.

But psychologically.

Stop interfering.

Let what you've built express itself.

源

Next: CHAPTER 11 — Coaching & Leading From the Inside-Out

Most coaching focuses on correcting behavior.
But behavior is downstream from mindset… and mindset is downstream from thought.
In the next chapter, you'll learn how the best leaders create calm, confidence, and accountability—not by controlling people… but by understanding how the mind works.

CHAPTER 11 — Coaching & Leading From the Inside-Out

At some point, every performer becomes a leader.

Maybe you become a team captain.
A parent.
A coach.
A manager.
A mentor.
A veteran who younger players look up to.

You may not have asked for the role...
...but leadership has a way of finding you.

And here's the truth:
Leadership shows up most clearly under pressure.

Pressure Doesn't Just Show Up in Performance

Most people think pressure is just a personal thing.
A performer thing.
A "mental game" thing.

But pressure doesn't only show up in performance.
It shows up in people.

It shows up in how they think.
How they speak.
How they listen.
How they relate.
How they lead.

When pressure rises, people don't just get tight physically...
they get tight mentally.

They get defensive.
They get reactive.
They get fearful.
They start protecting themselves.

And a leader can either add more meaning to that moment...
or create space for the noise to settle.

The Hidden Trap

Most leadership models are outside-in.

They focus on controlling behavior:

Motivate harder.
Push harder.
Demand more.
Fix the attitude.
Correct the mistake.

Raise your voice.
Apply pressure.

But when people already feel pressure…
adding more pressure rarely creates freedom.

It creates protection.

And protected people do not have freedom.

They don't communicate openly.
They don't learn quickly.
They don't take healthy risks.
They play "not to lose."

Which means the leader unintentionally becomes the source of interference…
even with good intentions.

Two Environments Every Leader Creates

Whether you realize it or not, what you do as a leader creates one of two environments:

> People tighten and protect themselves.
> or
> People relax and trust what they know.

This isn't about being "nice."

It's about being clear.

It's about understanding what the mind does under pressure.

Because when people are caught in insecure thinking... they hide.
When the mind feels threatened... it shrinks the world.
When people get lost in pressure-thinking... they stop trusting themselves.

But when people feel understood...
something incredible happens:

They settle.
They reset.
They execute.

The Insight

Inside-out leadership is not about controlling people.
It's about *understanding* people.

It's about knowing that human beings don't perform better because they're yelled into confidence.

They perform better when the noise settles...
and their training comes back online. Their clarity comes back online.

That's why the greatest leaders don't just teach skill...
they transmit stability.

Not by being perfect.
But by being present.

A leader doesn't have to fix everyone's thinking.
A leader doesn't have to remove pressure.

A leader simply needs to stop adding meaning.
Stop escalating emotion.
Stop feeding the storm.

Because your state sets the tone of the environment.

Feelings Are Information

When people get caught up in their thinking and drift into a low state of mind, they aren't thinking clearly.

They don't see options.
They don't see perspective.
They don't see consequences.

They make decisions they later regret...
 once their clarity returns.

That's why the way you feel matters.

In a way, your feeling is your north star.

It's not a problem.
It's information.

It's showing you the quality of your thinking in the moment.

And this is true not only for ourselves…
but for other people, too.

Which is one reason not to be so tough on others when they "behave badly."

Because more often than not…
they aren't showing their character.

They're showing their state of mind.

A Story That Proves Inside-Out Leadership

A woman I worked with years ago told me something that felt completely real to her:

"My boss hates me."

I didn't argue with her.
I knew she truly believed it.

But I also knew something deeper:

When people live in a low state of mind, they don't show up as their best selves.
 They show up as their *struggling selves.*

So I said to her:

"Nobody in clarity behaves that way. Only people who are suffering do."

She paused.

Then she admitted something important—her boss had a difficult personal life.
There was drama outside of work.
Stress. Conflict. Pressure.

Still, she kept returning to the same conclusion:

"He hates me."

Until one day something incredible happened.

She called me and said, "Ed... I LOVE my boss!"

I literally had to look at the phone to make sure it was her calling.

And here's the most interesting part:

Her boss didn't change.

But my client experienced him differently—
more helpful, more human, more loving.

Not because she forced positive thinking...

...but because her own thinking shifted.

And when her thinking shifted...
her entire experience of her boss shifted.

If that's not proof that our experience of life comes from the inside-out...
I don't know what is.

Your Invisible Edge

The greatest gift a leader can offer is not a perfect plan.

It's a calm mind.

And calm minds create elite execution.

That's inside-out leadership.

Not control.
Not intensity for intensity's sake.
But clarity.

Because clarity spreads.

And when clarity spreads...
people rise.

源

Next: CHAPTER 12 — The Game Within the Game (Ripple Effect)

What begins as a search for better performance often becomes something much bigger.

In the next chapter, you'll explore how this understanding ripples far beyond sports—and into the way you live.

CHAPTER 12 — The Game Within the Game (Ripple Effect)

Most people don't realize they're stepping into something much bigger.

They think they're learning how to play better.
How to handle pressure.
How to stay confident.
How to stop getting in their own way.

That's what brings them in.

But as their understanding deepens, something subtle begins to happen.

They notice they're not just calmer in competition.
They're calmer in life.

Not because they're trying to be.
Not because they've adopted a new philosophy.
But because they're starting to see how their experience actually works.

At first, they chalk it up to coincidence.

"Maybe I'm just having a good week."

But then it keeps happening.

They recover faster after mistakes.
They don't overthink as long.
They feel more present with their kids.
They don't carry work stress home as much.
They don't take things as personally.

Nothing about their circumstances has necessarily changed.

But something *fundamental* in their relationship with experience has.

They're no longer treating every thought as truth.
They're no longer assuming every emotion is a problem.
They're no longer fighting their inner world.

And without realizing it, they've begun *playing a different game*.

Not just the game on the field.
The game within the game.

At first, it shows up on the field.

An athlete notices they don't spiral as long after a mistake.
They settle faster between points.
They recover quicker after a bad inning.

Nothing magical.
Nothing forced.
Just less mental friction.

Then they start noticing it off the field.

An argument with a spouse doesn't hook them as deeply.
A stressful email doesn't ruin their entire day.
A bad commute doesn't feel personal anymore.

The volume of life quietly turns down.

Not because circumstances improve.
Not because they've mastered emotional control.
But because they're no longer assuming that every feeling means something is wrong.

They begin to see that emotions move the same way thoughts do.

They arise.
They pass.
They change.
They were never permanent.

Before this understanding, most people unknowingly treat uncomfortable emotions as emergencies.

If I feel anxious, something must be wrong.
If I feel discouraged, I must be broken.
If I feel unmotivated, I must need fixing.

That innocent misunderstanding creates a constant internal battle.

Fix this.
Change that.
Get rid of this feeling.
Try harder.

The battle itself becomes the real source of exhaustion.

As that misunderstanding falls away, something else becomes obvious:

Nothing is actually broken.

The human system is remarkably intelligent.

Just as your body knows how to digest food and heal cuts, your mind knows how to return to clarity.

It always has.

Most people simply learned to distrust it.

When that trust starts to come back online, life begins to feel lighter.

Not euphoric.
Not perfect.

Lighter.

There's more space around experiences.
More room to breathe.
More room to be human.

Parents begin to notice they're less reactive with their kids.

They still care.
They still guide.
They still set boundaries.

But there's less edge underneath it.
Less fear driving the interaction.

They don't need their children's behavior to determine their emotional state as much anymore.

They see moods come and go.
They see storms pass.
They stop personalizing every wave.

Which, interestingly, gives their children more space to regulate too.

I once saw this truth embodied in a way I'll never forget.

Basketball prospect Rayna DuBose once told me something that stopped me in my tracks.

Before she lost her arms and legs, she was heading in the wrong direction. Hanging out with the wrong people. No real sense of purpose.

Then her life changed overnight.

Today, Rayna is a motivational speaker. She's deeply at peace. She's never been happier.

Not in spite of what happened.
But because of the clarity it brought.

Rayna once shared that the first thing she does every morning is unplug her arms and legs from charging.

And yet, she lives with more aliveness, gratitude, and presence than most people I know that *do* have arms and legs.

She showed me something I'll never forget:

Happiness isn't created by circumstances.
It's revealed when we stop looking *outside* ourselves.

Her life didn't become easier.

Her relationship with experience became clearer.

And when that happens, suffering naturally falls away.

Not because life becomes perfect.

But because the inner argument with life ends.

Coaches notice they're calmer on the sidelines.

They don't feel responsible for controlling every outcome.
They communicate more simply.
More honestly.
More directly.
Without the emotional charge.

Players feel it immediately.

A calmer adult nervous system creates a calmer athletic environment.

At work, people notice they don't catastrophize as quickly.

A mistake is a mistake.
Feedback is feedback.
A bad meeting is a bad meeting.

Not a referendum on their worth.
Not a prediction of their future.
Not evidence that they're failing at life.

They still care about doing good work.

But they're no longer carrying the extra psychological weight.

This is what people are really discovering:

They don't live inside circumstances.
They live inside their moment-to-moment thinking.

And thinking is transient.
Always moving.
Always changing.

Which means their experience is also transient.
Always moving.
Always changing.

This realization quietly ends a lifelong habit:

Arguing with internal experience.

When you stop arguing with your mind, you suffer less.

Not because unpleasant thoughts disappear.
Not because hard emotions never show up.

But because you're no longer adding a second layer of resistance.

Pain may still happen.
Suffering decreases.

There's a difference.

Over time, people begin to describe themselves differently.

"I feel more like myself."
"I don't get stuck as long."
"I bounce back faster."
"I'm enjoying things more."

They didn't install positivity.
They didn't replace negative thoughts.
They didn't rewire their personality.

They simply stopped mistaking temporary internal weather for permanent reality.

And something deeper emerges.

A quiet okay-ness.

Not loud confidence.
Not constant happiness.

A steady sense that:

"I can handle life."

Because they see that life has always been moving through them.

They were never meant to micromanage it.

This is the game within the game.

The invisible shift beneath performance.

The understanding that frees athletes... and in the process, frees people.

Not into perfect lives.
Not into problem-free existence.

But into a more natural relationship with being human.

Less inner warfare.
More inner peace.

Less fixing.
More trusting.

Less gripping.
More allowing.

Elite performance may be what brought you here.

But what stays is something even bigger:

A better life.

源

Next: CHAPTER 13 — The Invisible Edge: A New Identity

At first, these principles feel like something you're learning. But eventually, it becomes something you *are*.

In the next chapter, we'll explore how true transformation happens—not by effort... but by understanding. And how that understanding creates a new identity you can trust under any pressure.

CHAPTER 13 — The Invisible Edge: A New Identity

At some point, it becomes obvious.

This was never really a performance book.

It was a *freedom* book.

Because the real breakdown was never on the court.
It was never in the moment.

It was in the misunderstanding of how experience works.

And once that misunderstanding starts to dissolve…

Performance improves.
But something bigger happens.

Life feels different.

Lighter.
Simpler.
More workable.

Not because circumstances change.
Not because problems disappear.

But because *you're no longer living inside a misunderstanding.*

This Was Never About Doing More

Most performers grow up believing the answer is more.

More discipline.
More grit.
More strategies.
More visualization.
More control.

But clarity doesn't come from effort.

Flow doesn't come from force.

At some point, it becomes clear:

Nothing new needs to be added.

Something simply needs to be seen.

And once it's seen...

You don't just change what you do.

You begin to recognize who you've always been.

A New Identity (That You Didn't Create)

When these ideas are new, they sound like concepts.

Interesting.
Hopeful.
Worth exploring.

But over time, they stop feeling like ideas.

They start feeling like **truth**.

Not the truth of someone who has it all figured out.

The quieter truth of someone who sees what's real…

…and what is simply thought.

You begin to notice things.

Pressure isn't coming from the situation.
Confidence isn't a possession.
Clarity doesn't need to be manufactured.
Thought isn't a command.
Feelings aren't instructions.
Ability doesn't vanish.

Nothing fundamental is ever lost.

Access simply comes and goes.

As these realizations deepen, something shifts.

You don't panic when confidence dips.

You don't make meaning out of every emotion.

You don't treat nerves as a problem.

You don't assume something is wrong when experience gets uncomfortable.

Not because you're "better at the mental game"…

But because you *understand* what you're looking at.

And understanding changes the relationship.

Before you realize it, you're living from a different place.

You're operating from a different place.

Not a new personality.

Not a new persona.

A more honest one.

Freedom Is Space

Freedom doesn't mean a quiet mind.

It doesn't mean no pressure.

It doesn't mean no emotion.

It means space.

Space between you and what you're experiencing.

Space to notice a thought without following it.

Space to feel intensity without needing to fix it.

Space to let internal weather move.

And in that space…

You find yourself again.

You find presence.

You find what you've trained to do.

You find the moment.

Not because you forced your way there.

But because nothing was *blocking* it anymore.

The Invisible Edge

The Invisible Edge was never a trick.

Never a hack.

Never a routine.

It's a quiet understanding that becomes the ground you stand on.

That's why it's invisible.

It doesn't look like trying.

It doesn't look like effort.

It looks like simplicity.

It looks like ease.

It looks like a mind that has stopped fighting itself.

And when the mind stops fighting itself...

Elite execution becomes natural again.

Not an Ending — A Recognition

This doesn't feel like an ending.

It feels like a recognition.

Because clarity changes perspective.
And with new perspective, we never return to our old selves.

If parts of this book resonated with you, it isn't because I gave you something.

It's because you recognized something.

Something you already knew at a deeper level.

Now you simply see it more clearly.

And clarity tends to keep unfolding.

Not through force.
Not through effort.

But through lived experience.

This understanding will continue to deepen on its own.

And as it does...

It won't just influence how you perform.

It will quietly shape how you move through life.

How you respond.
How you relate.
How you show up.

One Last Thing...

Trying too hard has a cost.

Physically, we understand this.

Overtrain the body and it breaks down.

The same is true mentally.

When the mind becomes a project...

When performance becomes something to manufacture...

People create tension.

They create burnout.

They create self-judgment.

Not because they're weak.

But because they're working from a misunderstanding.

Elite performance has never been built through force.

It has always emerged from understanding.

Understanding opens the door.

This book was simply meant to point toward it.

I genuinely believe that if more people understood what you've just explored, there would be far less unnecessary suffering in the world.

Not because life would become perfect.

But because people would stop being at war with their own experience.

Your best is not missing.

It's only ever covered by *thought*.

And thought settles.

Not by force.

But by understanding.

Your best has always been inside you.

And it always will be...

That's the Invisible Edge.

Calm mind.
Elite execution.

APPENDIX A

THE CHARACTERS CHEAT SHEET

Quick reference for athletes, parents, and coaches

These "characters" are not problems to fix.

They are normal thought patterns that show up when we care. Once you recognize them, they lose their power—because you stop treating them like truth.

THE EVALUATOR

Catchphrase: "Not good enough."
Signature move: Turns performance into judgment.
Cost: Tightness, fear, self-consciousness.
Reminder: Commentary isn't truth.

THE MIND READER

Catchphrase: "They think I..."
Signature move: Assumes others' thoughts with zero evidence.

Cost: Anxiety, overthinking, people-pleasing.
Reminder: Your mind is guessing, not knowing.

THE FORTUNE TELLER

Catchphrase: "This is going to go bad."
Signature move: Predicts failure before it happens.
Cost: Hesitation, playing not-to-lose.
Reminder: The future isn't a fact.

THE HISTORIAN

Catchphrase: "Remember last time?"
Signature move: Replays past mistakes.
Cost: Loss of present-moment freedom.
Reminder: The past isn't happening now.

THE CONTROL FREAK

Catchphrase: "I need to feel ready first."
Signature move: Demands certainty before action.
Cost: Over-control, tension, stuckness.
Reminder: Freedom comes before confidence.

THE SPOTLIGHT OPERATOR

Catchphrase: "Everyone is watching."
Signature move: Turns moments into public judgment.
Cost: Self-consciousness and avoidance.
Reminder: Most people are thinking about themselves.

THE PERFECTIONIST

Catchphrase: "Perfect or worthless."
Signature move: Makes mistakes unacceptable.
Cost: Pressure, fear of failure.
Reminder: Excellence requires freedom.

THE COMPARER

Catchphrase: "They're better than you."
Signature move: Turns life into rankings.
Cost: Insecurity, jealousy, playing small.
Reminder: Comparison kills rhythm.

THE TRAGEDIAN

Catchphrase: "This is a disaster."
Signature move: Turns a 2/10 problem into a 12/10 emergency.
Cost: Panic, spiraling, emotional exhaustion.
Reminder: Your voice weighs zero pounds—even when it acts like an Olympian with telenovela drama.

CORE REMINDER

The voices are not the source of performance—they're temporary thought *pretending* to be reality. When you see this clearly, you naturally return to calm and elite performance.

Continue the Work

If this book resonated with you, you don't need to do anything special.

Just play. Just live.

When pressure rises, you'll remember.
When thinking gets loud, you'll see it.
When clarity returns, you'll trust it.

Not because you practiced a technique...

...but because you've discovered the source.

(Source)

About the Author

Ed Tseng is a mental performance coach who helps athletes and high performers unlock elite performance through an inside-out understanding. A best-selling author, TEDx speaker, and Pro of the Year, Ed has worked with performers across sports, business, and life to simplify the mental game and help people thrive under pressure.

His work focuses on showing performers how the mind works—so they can stop interfering and let their training take over when it matters most.

Ed lives in Lawrenceville, New Jersey with his two children, Ava and Max. Together, they proudly started the **Tseng Legacy Foundation**, a family-led foundation supporting individuals in need and organizations doing meaningful work. *A portion of the author's royalties support the Tseng Legacy Foundation.*

To learn more about coaching, speaking, and resources:

Visit: EdTseng.com

Email: Ed@EdTseng.com

Instagram: @invisedgeperf

www.ingramcontent.com/pod-product-compliance
Lightning Source LLC
Chambersburg PA
CBHW050912160426
43194CB00011B/2370